Support the Caregiver

9 Strategies for Turning the Stress of Caregiving into Transformational Growth

Dr. David Davis

Joko Gilbert

<u>Table of Contents</u>

"If you're going through hell, keep going!" – Winston Churchill

Introduction

"The most beautiful people we have known are those who have known defeat, known suffering, known struggle, known loss, and have found their way out of those depths" - Elisabeth Kübler-Ross

These 9 Strategies are for caregivers of people with Alzheimer's disease and other dementias. While the principles contained within these pages are applicable to so many of the circumstances of our lives, the need in this moment, is to address the concerns of the caregiver, and more specifically, those of us who are taking care of a Loved One who is afflicted with Alzheimer's. This is not a book about the disease itself, addressing instead the specific challenges that a caregiver for an afflicted Loved One goes through.

I know what you know and I feel what you feel. I know that it is one of, if not the most difficult challenges a person will ever have to face in their entire lives. I know that it has the ability to take so much away from us, including, but certainly not limited to, our health, our financial resources, our dreams, our happiness. It compromises our relationships with our friends and families; it exhausts us and tests our mettle in a way that has probably not been tested before. It is painfully slow and exhausting, and it is constantly changing, causing us to have to adapt to ever shifting and worsening circumstances. Our identities perish, forcing us to have to redefine ourselves in a way we could never have imagined. Our laughter grows more feeble, our ability to see the beauty in a sunset becomes diminished and our sense of wonder for life becomes muted.

In short, we change, because as caregivers our entire focus can't help but shift as someone we love grows more and more helpless. What can be more heartbreaking than watching someone whom you love, who has been an integral part of your life, as they disappear into a place where you can no longer reach them, yet they stand right in front of you? How sad is it to witness your mother who brought you into this world, or your father, who taught you how to ride a bicycle, or your spouse, whose eyes you looked into when you said your vows, when they no longer remember who you are?

My advice for my son when he was younger, was that life is sacred and to be savored, but it can be *challenging* at times. I wanted to protect him from the rough edges of growing up, however, despite my best efforts, that simply is not how life works. The best Strategies involve learning how to adapt to the stresses, and even lean into them in a way that they become fuel for growth and understanding. Inevitably, we will be challenged and traumatized at various times, and cultivating the right mindset will contribute to the kind of wisdom that allows us to see life for what it is, in its entirety. Life is indeed a sacred trust, no matter the slings and arrows that we must endure. And we must guard it well, with the full measure of our abilities.

I can say without reservation, that there has never been a personal challenge in my life, as great as being the caregiver to my wife Linda, diagnosed with Alzheimer's at the young age of fifty one. Nothing could have prepared me for the hardships I would have to endure, or to travel to the far reaches of my inner landscape where I would search for understanding. I just knew, after the initial shock wore off, that I was determined to have this be an experience of growth, knowing that there was a great opportunity to come out of this with a deeper understanding of myself and a way to translate that into a more meaningful and fulfilling life.

The 9 Strategies are timeless and changeless and have an unlimited power to transform lives. The 9 Strategies remain a constant in that they redirect us to what is timeless and changeless within ourselves. Joko and I studied so many of the resources available to caregivers and adapted those which we thought were the most effective and transformative. Truly transformative living is about a *"coming home"* to rest in the most fundamental nature of ourselves. It is not about adding more things to our already cluttered lives. Rather, it is about stripping away what prevents us from negotiating life with serenity and equanimity. For the caregiver, it is about putting the circumstances of our challenges into a broader perspective, so that we can recognize that in the midst of struggle, is the path to peace. In Buddhism, they say that there are two kinds of suffering: the kind that leads to more suffering and the kind that leads to the end of suffering.

While I will clearly and methodically outline the 9 Strategies, the recommendation is that you choose any or all of them that resonate with *you*.

When faithfully and diligently applied, they can bring us, the caregivers, to a place of purpose and fulfillment. We should endeavor to be as sober and realistic about this process as possible. Remember that there is no substitute for being deeply engaged. Recognize this as an opportunity for growth and empowerment, which can be quite difficult at times. And also, recognize that because Alzheimer's is a terminal illness, we want to come through this with the best parts of ourselves still intact. We want to create a compelling enough reason for ourselves to not just survive caregiving, but thrive as a result of it. The opportunity to cultivate the attributes of patience, empathy, love, understanding, gratitude, inner strength, faith, courage and wisdom are greatest when they are forged in the fires of a struggle of this magnitude. We can never pretend or presume, that just because we are *open* to such potent teachings that the process is made any easier. It certainly isn't! In caregiving quitting isn't an option. Somedays it is simply about searching for the courage to put one foot in front of the other, while on other days you discover that your well of compassion has become so deep, it's actually beginning to feel like a reason for optimism.

The greatest teachers come to us in the dark, and caregiving can be a lonely, dark place. No matter the sincerity of support, or closeness of the community you have to lean on, at the end of the day, it is your head alone that takes its rest on the pillow in the somber shadows cast by the moonlight outside your window. It is your fears and hopes, and tears and smiles that keep you company in your solitude. It is precisely at moments like these that you must stand vigilant at the gates of your own mind and heart, refusing audience to all of the emotions, habits and thoughts that will undermine your resolve so essential for your personal growth during this time. Wisdom lies in creating those distinctions for yourself. Your healing comes from treating yourself with love and reverence at a time when exhaustion and despair taunt you.

These 9 Strategies offer you a light on the path of growth. I started out by saying that I am a caregiver. Like you, I understand the suffering of this dreadful illness. I also understand the yearning to live a life that is filled with contentment and possibility. Life is indeed precious, and we owe it to our Loved Ones and to ourselves to take a swan dive into the deep end of the pool of possibilities and to be a shining example of how to grow and prosper emotionally through our profound challenges.

I am giving myself permission to stretch my spiritual beliefs and ask that they not alienate you but inspire you to examine yours and apply them in any way that works for you. For caregiving to be a healing journey towards transformation, I believe with all my heart that it must be a spiritual quest. It is not enough to have steely resolve as a caregiver. Doing what needs to be done by placing one foot in front of the other will get you to your destination. I am asking you to arrive at your destination as a better version of yourself. *Our destination is a future filled with the quiet joy earned from approaching our hardships with a newly cultivated understanding.* During caregiving, something deep inside us must fundamentally shift, bringing us to a place where our lives are embracing possibility.

The Buddhist philosopher, Pema Chödrön said, *"Only to the extent that we expose ourselves to annihilation can that which is indestructible be found in us"*. Being a caregiver can destroy us, or it can resurrect us into a life of wisdom and compassion.

When Linda was diagnosed, both of us embarked on a journey that would reshape our destinies. To search the depths of my pain and thus discover empathy, patience, understanding and love is the path to my healing. It is my strong desire for those who share this journey with me to experience hope and inspiration, in a community of love and support, that by our choice, can be *Positively Transforming*.

Dr. David Davis

www.supportthecaregiver.com

Strategy 1: Eliminate the Negatives

"We shall draw from the heart of suffering itself the means of inspiration and survival" - Winston Churchill

We are born as empty vessels, with possibility as the blank slate on which our lives are written. From the moment our consciousness begins to wind itself into the fabric of its environment, we become imprinted with all that we come into contact with, utilizing all of our senses. This continues until an age where we begin to be cognizant of our own identity as volitional beings, free to take the world and make it into our own image.

Ah, if only it were all that simple. During the years of imprinting, we are heavily under the influence of our mothers, fathers, teachers and preachers, all of whom have their very tidy ideas about who they think we should be and they devote entire lives and careers telling us how to think. Fortunately, in the hands of people with a degree of awareness, the majority of information passed on to us is useful and designed to keep us safe, morally upright, and for the most part, out of trouble. However, it appears that all of these well meaning people also bring to the table their fears and insecurities and whether by design or by happenstance, we learn these attitudes and behaviors as well. So before we have a chance to fully create an identity of our own that is congruent with who we are born to be, we frequently take on the dialogue of too much negativity, doubt and fear and these become a large part of the inner resources available to deal with challenges throughout our lives. And fear is a far greater challenge to overcome than the circumstances that are the object of our fear. Recognizing then, that we are the product of all of the influences and choices we have made in our lives, we find ourselves at a very opportune moment to lay the foundation of self awareness.

The mind is a rather valuable little lump of clay, so we must not underestimate it or think it ordinary. There is nothing quite like the mind, for the whole universe becomes real for us by means of the mind. The mind bears fruit according to your thoughts. From the mind can come peace, illusion, intelligence, humor. The blessing of the mind can make you a poet, an intellectual, an artist or a musician. You can earn a degree with it, or you can be transformed by it.

If the mind is corrupted, it will always cause trouble; it will spoil whatever you do and ruin your path to healing and transformation. Take care of your mind. It is a friend which will bring you happiness.

I often reflect on my time as a caregiver. Linda was diagnosed in 2009. To say that my mind has travelled the extreme range of emotions would be vast understatement. To say that I have not experienced deep wells of anger, resentment, sadness and depression would be a lie. I have been angry at Linda, I have been angry at God, I have been angry at myself. I have watched the way I interact with the world go from being lighthearted and relatively carefree to terse and sometimes downright antagonistic. My sense of humor has atrophied as I saw my dreams, hopes and desires deform into something that I could not have imagined or planned for. To say the least, I became quite negative. I tried to stay positive, however negativity usually won out in the battle of my tumultuous mind.

We have to begin in the beginning although we do so with the end result in mind. And the end result is the oft repeated common thread throughout this book, that we want to replace a version of post traumatic stress syndrome with post traumatic *growth* syndrome. Even though technically, this might not be considered post traumatic in the traditional sense of a single, or series of specific trauma's, try telling your nervous system that it hasn't been traumatized when you first heard the doctor diagnose your spouse, parent or friend with Alzheimer's disease. The trauma is very real, and it plots a course like any other life altering event, deep into the fabric of your emotional self, throwing your whole system into conflict. The mind is a miraculous and brilliant creation of nature, one of whose primary instincts is to protect itself from destruction. So when a set of circumstances come along that threaten its sense of the familiar and the comfortable, all bets are off, and what follows is a mad dash to try to make sense of a new and unfamiliar reality.

Welcome to the strange and topsy turvy world of caregiving. Perhaps it can be said that your initiation into caregiving began the moment you heard the diagnosis roll off your doctors lips in slow motion through a pea soup fog of shock and disbelief. Or perhaps it came when you first noticed with suspicion that your wife asked you the same question she had asked not even sixty seconds prior. But whenever your initiation came, you remember that moment as life changing and future re-defining. And, it was in that moment that a cascade of choices began to covertly wend their way into your world of possibilities. We were then faced with choices about the logistics of how we care for our Loved One, as well as how we *personally*, were going to deal with such a radical shift in our circumstances.

So this, then becomes a great place to begin, because for any new possibility to take root, there must be room for it. And the most cluttered room in our house is typically the one between our ears. Nothing can happen of any real benefit, until we take a step back, gather perspective, and explore not just our options, but the internal resources we have available to us. The usual questions like "why me?" or "why her?", will be asked almost reflexively. As soon as possible we need to recognize that some questions only serve to keep us mired in negative emotions where nobody wins. We must courageously learn to ask new questions, the answers to which can mean the difference between a caregiver sacrificing his own health, or moving through this process with a deeper sense of well-being.

Current statistics from the Alzheimer's Association inform us that approximately 63% of caregivers will die before their Loved Ones afflicted with the illness due to both the stress involved and ignoring their own health care needs for the needs of their Loved One.

Begin the process of cleaning house by eliminating negative self talk and replacing it with uplifting, inspiring thoughts. If you find yourself experiencing a sense of hopelessness or powerlessness, you know that this is a particularly useful place for you to begin. Negativity doesn't change things. It keeps you stuck. So change your thoughts and begin to take stock in what you appreciate in your life, not what you don't like. Remember that you are clearing the *stinking thinking* out of your mind that has not served you. Avoid the company of people who bring you down and seek out the company of people who nurture you. Your abilities as a caregiver and your ability to stay physically, emotionally and mentally healthy are greatly compromised when your mind is infested with thoughts that contribute to your resentment, frustration, depression, worry and fear. You want to clear out space inside and begin to fill it with the seeds of your own healing. The goal of these 9 Strategies is nothing short of using a time of grief and sadness to honestly access the most heroic aspects of yourself. Self-talk can make or break your life! It has been said, "Whether you think you can, or think you can't… either way, you're right." Argue for your limitations and they become yours.

In the latest Rocky movie, "Creed"(yes, I have seen every Rocky movie!), Rocky Balboa was training his young fighter to do battle with the toughest boxer in the world, and he stood him in front of his own image in the mirror and said, "You see this guy here? That's the toughest opponent you're ever going to have to face. I believe that's true in the ring, and I think that's true in life. Now show me something".

In the cartoon strip, Pogo said, "We have met the enemy and he is us".

There is a dialogue that takes place inside of us, and in all likelihood has gone on for much of our lives, that severely undermines our greatness. I say dialogue and not a monologue, because we respond to it; we have discourse with it; we are in compliance with it by virtue of the fact that we have bestowed authority upon it. Sadly, and all too often, it tells us not how great we are but how we fall short. It is a mythical voice whose authority is no more based in the reality of our lives than the stories it makes up about us. Stories like we are are not worthy, we are not smart enough, good looking enough, talented enough, prosperous enough. We consign ourselves to its declarations as the truth we must sculpt ourselves to. So we become the reflected image of the voice of negativity within us, which could end up being the costliest of all crimes. We deny from ourselves the possibility of expansive joy, we turn our back to our own dreams of possibility and potential, we lose the very sacredness of life and hold it captive with a ransom that is beyond our reach. And it is all a lie that we live and die on, and spend enormous sums of energy justifying and defending that belief.

We, by our very nature are indomitable and no less spectacular than the sun. Einstein said, "God is subtle, but not malicious", so if we are in the dark about our place in the world, it simply is because we are not paying attention. There is a much subtler voice that rings furtively behind the din of our negative incantations of stunted self esteem, that actually is vying for our attention. It is the voice of our divine nature that wants nothing more than to remind us of all that we are and can be. That you are without limit, save *that* which is self imposed or physical. It is, if you pay attention, *your* voice. It is you, seeking expression beyond the bill of goods you sold yourself.

We ice the cake of our negativity with the daily musings of television, newspapers and conversations with people who have traded in the optimism of a life consciously lived for the prevalent hum of fear and cynicism that seems to have taken root all around us. A person has only to switch on a television to witness every inhumane act possible, either on the news or television shows that only serve to sensationalize.

According to the A.C. Nielsen Co., the average American watches more than 4 hours of television each day (or 28 hours per week, or 2 months of nonstop TV-watching per year). In a 65-year life, that person will have spent 9 years glued to the tube. Does it really take a scientific study to conclude that 9 years of television over the course of a lifetime is not time well spent? Imagine the outcome, not just on an individual, but on an entire society, if those 4 hours per day were spent on self-improvement?

We have forgotten, that life is so much bigger than the wholesale traders in fear and sensationalism would have us believe. Life, at its core is about nature, beauty, art, music and love, all of which are infiltrated by the rich tapestry of humanity. We have the resources of all of creation, both natural and manmade to call upon in our understanding of the world around us and more specifically, how to successfully meet the challenges that now present themselves to us with great ferocity.

I have witnessed so many caregivers who have become fractionalized, marginalized and emotionally paralyzed because of what they have not yet realized. Life, even with all of its challenges, never ceases to be an opportunity to tap into the humanity we speak of. *As caregivers, it becomes incumbent upon us to put blinders on to all which does not serve us in our quest to be emotionally prosperous during such an enormous challenge.* Our greatest resolve should be to stand strong and vigilant at the gates of our own consciousness, unwilling to let anything pass through that seeks to undermine our resolve. Taking care of someone with Alzheimer's puts an enormous strain on our resources and the only choice that makes any sense, is to immerse ourselves into those behaviors, those ideas that serve to strengthen our ability to emerge whole and healthy. *Eliminating Negatives means to create distinctions for ourselves as to what we choose to involve ourselves in, or with whom, for that matter.*

One evening, an elderly Cherokee Brave told his grandson about a battle that goes on inside people. He said, "my son, the battle is between two wolves inside us all. One is evil. It is anger, envy, jealousy, sorrow, regret, greed, arrogance, self-pity, guilt, resentment, inferiority, lies, false pride, superiority and ego. The other is good. It is joy, peace, love, hope, serenity, humility, kindness, benevolence, empathy, generosity, truth, compassion and faith." The grandson thought about it for a minute and then asked his grandfather: "Which wolf wins?" The old Cherokee simply replied, "the one that you feed."

As caregivers we are already leaning into the sharp edges of life. We have before us an opportunity to forge a life of compassion, patience, wisdom, courage and love. If we simply feed and nurture the best virtues within us, we can move through this experience profoundly healthier for it.

The author of the classic text, *On Death and Dying*, Elisabeth Kübler-Ross defined five clear stages of grief that people go through when they experience loss. The five stages, denial, anger, bargaining, depression and acceptance are a part of the framework that makes up our learning to live with what or whom we have lost. The stages have evolved since their introduction over three decades ago. Her co-researcher, David Kessler explains that "they were never meant to help tuck messy emotions into neat packages. They are responses to loss that many people have, but there is not a typical response to loss as there is no typical loss. Our grief is as individual as our lives. They are tools to help us frame and identify what we may be feeling. But they are not stops on some linear timeline of grief. Not everyone goes through all of them or in a prescribed order. Our hope is that with these stages comes the knowledge of grief's terrain, making us better equipped to cope with life and loss. At times, people in grief will often report more stages. Just remember your grief is as unique as you are".

My strong contention is that we get to choose by being aware of where we are at in the process. Stages of grief are not something that we fall victim to. Rather they are, as mentioned earlier, our way of coping and protecting ourselves.

By being aware, conscious, and perhaps above all, willing, we have the opportunity to chart our own course through the tumultuous stages of grief, emerging from each with a more profound understanding of ourselves and the deep emotional satisfaction and peace that comes from such hard fought wisdom. This is not about positive thinking. I have run across countless people who are negative to the core, who pepper their conversations with idle and empty sunny assertions that seem to have little to no affect on the trajectory of their lives. The process of Eliminating the Negatives is quite literally just that. Taking an emotional and intelligent inventory of the thoughts, patterns and behaviors that have shaped us thus far and utilizing the resources and technologies available to eliminate the ones that have not served us, and replacing them with ones that do. There must be a fundamental shift not just in *what* we think, but *how* we think.

Being a caregiver to a Loved One with Alzheimer's, as I will say again and again, is one of the most challenging experiences anyone will have. It requires rolling up our sleeves, and with self-acceptance and gentle perseverance, self love and self respect, embracing the possibilities, rather than surrendering or falling victim to a default life of brokenness.

In her book, *Broken Open*, Elizabeth Lesser tells us, "Adversity is a natural part of being human. It is the height of arrogance to prescribe a moral code or health regime or spiritual practice as an amulet to keep things from falling apart. Things do fall apart. It is in their nature to do so. When we try to protect ourselves from the inevitability of change, we are not listening to the soul. We are listening to our fear of life and death, our smaller egos will to prevail. To listen to your soul is to stop fighting with your life, to stop fighting when things fall apart, when they don't go our way, when we get sick, when we are betrayed or mistreated or misunderstood. To listen to the soul is to slow down, to feel deeply, to see yourself clearly, to surrender to discomfort in uncertainty and to wait."

Meaningful and useful growth must be expansive and inclusive, which contradicts our idea of spirituality as cloistered and contracted. We perceive spirituality as being uniquely inner directed when in truth it must become outer directed in equal measure. Otherwise, of what value is it, if it doesn't more fully integrate us into the world?

My old mindset was that Linda's illness had assaulted me. I have been charged at, and I have been flanked, and the attrition rate is staggering, as my presumptions about myself lay dead or dying. My entire life I have felt as if there was more to me, untapped, unwritten, unsung. It has been a source of constant sorrow and frustration, in part because there was no one to hold responsible but myself. And now I can focus blame like a laser in the direction of Linda and her illness, because I surely would have broken out of my hardened seed and blossomed had it not been for her illness, right? And now, I have come to understand and appreciate that the mind has this remarkable ability to redirect thought traffic until things line up in a way that brings objective truth to light. Simply by recognizing how the dark tendencies of unchecked thought create a cascade effect of negativity is truly a first step in shifting how we think. Sorrow becomes gratitude; fear becomes optimism; frustration becomes patience, blame becomes wisdom and resentment becomes love.

Eliminating the Negatives makes room for a much higher order of expression where creativity can flourish and all of those untapped and unwritten avenues of possibility find new outlets.

Strategy 2: Meditation

"In the midst of movement and chaos, keep stillness inside of you" - Deepak Chopra

It can be said that meditation is like fly fishing; easy to do, difficult to master. It can also be said, that even in its most rudimentary form, the benefits are profound and any effort put forth will yield bountiful fruit.

I started meditating in 1982, and I recall how difficult it was at first. While the simple act of sitting still wasn't particularly challenging, getting my mind to quiet itself was like trying to relax on a roller coaster. It just seemed to run counter to having years of incessant inner chatter as the expected norm. I didn't even consider that a tumultuous mind had the ability to quiet itself. However, with instruction, I created a meditation area, and I sat every day; sometimes for just a few minutes and on occasion, I would sit for a whole hour. During that time, I would do my best to focus on anything that would distract my mind from itself and bring it into a pointed focus of serenity. What became apparent quickly was that meditation would open up a feeling of *space* inside me, or an openness where before there was only noise. That feeling began to carry into the rest of my day, as I felt calmer, and even more creative.

As time passed on, the simple act of sitting to meditate felt less like a chore as I would find myself slipping almost effortlessly into a state of inner calm. I now look forward to it, as it feels almost like a vacation from all of the unnecessary mental clutter. Sometimes, I actually *fall* into meditation, where my mind just seems to collapse in on itself, almost of its own accord, and there I am, in the center of a warm and peaceful void, where the doors are barred from any negativity, or useless noise. There is only space and possibility, and it feels like a place where I belong. A place from which I could move forward into the world with only what was needed for life to feel sweet.

In its simplest form, meditation is a vacation from your mind and one of the most powerful tools in the caregiver's arsenal as well as one of the greatest gifts you can give yourself. It is a process of sitting quietly and witnessing how your mind works. The value in this is developing the ability to reign in your never ending barrage of constant inner dialogue.

The Buddhist teacher, Sogyal Rinpoche tells us, *"We don't know who we really are, or what aspects of ourselves we should identify with or believe in. So many contradictory voices, dictates, and feelings fight for control over our inner lives that we find ourselves scattered everywhere, in all directions, leaving nobody at home. Meditation, then, is bringing the mind home. Slowly you will become a master of your own bliss, a chemist of your own joy, with all sorts of remedies always at hand to elevate, cheer, illuminate, and inspire your every breath and movement. What is a great spiritual practitioner? A person who lives always in the presence of his or her own true self, someone who has found and who uses continually the springs and sources of profound inspiration."*

Just like exercising your muscles, the more you do this, the stronger your ability becomes. And the result is that you have created open, quiet, peaceful space within yourself, where you can begin to paint a new picture of your life.

As caregivers, we have been charged with taking on more than our typical share of the world. We must nurture our lives and all of its needs and of course, take care of another life as well. Not unlike parenting, but at a time in our lives when we thought we were done changing diapers, and cutting food into bite size pieces. One of the main emotional differences between parenting and caregiving is, with parenting all of our actions are tempered by the expectation and excitement of watching our child grow into a healthy independent adult. Obviously, not so in caregiving. There is no such temperance, only the despair of knowing that all of our actions will be met with a continued decline into an end of life scenario. Hardly a cause for enthusiasm.

We must explore a way to disrupt the pattern of negative energy and the malignant influence it has over us. More importantly, we do this by changing what we identify with from the at times limited, claustrophobic burden of caregiving, to the recognition that we are in fact much greater in scope and perspective than our circumstances. Through the power of meditation we can see our lives for how big they are, and identify with the possibilities that arise from regular practice. *Meditation is that powerful!* In a sentence, it turns off the faucet of negativity and limitation, and opens up the floodgates of peace and possibility.

In the classic Tibetan Book of Living and Dying, we are asked to *"never underestimate meditation. Meditation is the heart of all spiritual practice, the master key to knowledge, the stream of love, the sacrificial rite that earns the richness of grace".*

In this classic text, Sogyal Rinpoche goes on to say, *"The idea of meditation should not frighten you because, in your daily life, you already perform many kinds of meditation; it simply happens. Your skills and talents are perfected solely through meditation. Without one-pointed attention, is it possible for a doctor to administer to illness, a judge to make his decision, a professor to give a lecture? Without concentration, can one cook food, drive a car, keep a rhythm in music, solve mathematical problems? A degree of meditation is required to achieve anything. But in all these things, your meditation is directed toward the world, not towards your Inner Self. Just as you have occupied your mind with mundane activities, in the same way, to immerse the mind in love for your Inner Self, your divine nature, is meditation".*

We recognize progress as our mind becomes more peaceful and free from distractions. So often, especially early on, when Linda would ask me the same question over and over, my frustration would yield to a sense of calm that I recognize was a result of my regular meditation practice.

Caregiving is a circumstance that begs us to find a way to remain calm, present, and to be able to function "above the fray". How perfect that meditation gives us that gift!

For a caregiver, that open space inside of us where we know peacefulness becomes narrower, edging out the light until we flail around in the dim fog of chaos, desperately feeling around for something to grasp onto, something familiar, that can mete out morsels of comfort, if only for a while. So with the open, quiet, peaceful space that you create within yourself, you can begin to bring a sense of ease back into your life. The magic of opening up that space, that space which is within all of us, is revelatory.

When I sit down at my desk or in my study and it is cluttered, I simply cannot be productive. I feel a sense of unease and distractedness. Once my study or desk is clean and clear, my mind comes into sharper focus and productivity and creativity can begin to flow with much greater ease. Meditation is the clearing out the clutter of your mind, of everything that accumulates whether over a lifetime or even just over the past few minutes. Most importantly, it helps to understand your own mind.

Before we start meditating, we don't give much thought to what was going on inside our heads — it would just happen. Our mind can lead us to wherever it wants to go and too often we would follow its commands like an automaton. With time, we become aware of what's going on. We can make choices about how we respond to the impulses of our mind. And in understanding ourselves better, we are awarded increased flexibility and freedom.

If viewed as just a stress reliever, I would still maintain that it is of extraordinary value. Meditation is only getting warmed up when you first begin to practice it. It's like having a sports car that you never drive faster than 30 mph when its capabilities far exceed the limits you have placed on it. Meditation is a foundational practice for most if not all of the great spiritual teachings and religions of the world. Something quite magical can happen when the mind become still and the volume on our chatty voice starts to turn down towards zero.

It is said in many holy texts, like the Vedas, the Upanishads and even in the writings of Christian and Jewish theologians, that what is left in the quiet space of meditation is an experience of the divine, or God if you are so inclined. It's like God has been sitting there quietly waiting for you to sweep out the rubbish and the distractions to become more intimately known by you. If practiced with discipline and intention, over time, the ability to meditate becomes easier until you can almost effortlessly slip into meditation whenever you want.

I have recommended meditation as a practice to many of my patients throughout the years. Often times I have done so as a way for them to deal with the obvious stressors in their lives and I have also often presented it as a spiritual practice if I felt there was receptivity to that idea. So many people will tell me that they have "tried" to meditate, but it didn't work. They have listened to tapes, read books, been instructed, and yet, the busy, chatty mind always has a way of winning out over the simple desire for stillness. Isn't the mind a funny thing? It fights so hard for its own preservation that it will wage a battle against your simple request for it to rest for a short while. I find it humorous that one of the most effective techniques in beginning meditation is telling the mind what you want it to do when it is misbehaving. When it persists on insinuating itself into your moments of quiet, you actually have to tell it, like an intrusive party crasher, "not now, I am meditating; I will speak with you later. Be quiet!"

Make meditation a daily habit, whether it is for 5 minutes or one hour, and you will notice how other habits, thoughts and behaviors will all begin to change. There are so many moments during the course of Linda's illness when calmness prevailed in the midst of chaos. Whether she was hell bent on wandering off of our property, or hiding things around the house, like my shoes, I would stay surprisingly serene, settling into the calm place in the center of the storm. My ability to behave this way, only became easier with continued meditation.

Meditation is one of the cornerstone of the 9 Strategies for Caregivers. If you have been meditating for a while, and you feel comfortable with it, then feel free to skip this part. So … I highly recommend this as a daily habit. And while I'm not saying it's easy, you can start simply with just a few minutes and increase your time as you get better with practice. Don't expect to be good at it at first — that's why it's called "practice"!

1. Sit for just five minutes. Start with just five minutes a day, for as long as it takes for you to feel comfortable with it. There is no right or wrong time. Find a quiet place in your home, preferably the same place every day. By having a specific place to return to each time, you become comfortable and familiar with that spot and you associate that place with your practice of meditation. That space will take on a "special" meaning, your meditative energy will begin to accumulate, aiding you each time you sit for meditation. It is essential that you are comfortable, so do what is necessary to be easy on your body. Use a pillow to sit on, or several small pillows under your knees if you are sitting cross legged on the floor; you can have your back against a surface for support. If you are not comfortable on the floor, sit in a chair or on a couch. Rest your forearms on your thighs, feet parallel to each other on the floor. You want a natural and healthy upright posture. Whether you are sitting cross legged on the floor or in a chair, place your hands so that your pointing finger and thumb are touching, creating a circle, palms down or up, whichever you prefer. Approach this as a sacred ritual, your sacred ritual, deserving of your care and attention. As time goes on, and you feel the beneficial effects, increase your time in meditation. You can either set a little timer near you, or you can simply meditate until you "come out of meditation". Being able to meditate comfortably for a longer time will make you a very strong and capable meditator. What an amazing talent to have in your world of caregiving!

2. Meditate first thing each morning. It's easy to say, "I'll meditate every day," but then we forget to do it. Instead, set a reminder and put up a few strategically placed notes around your home that say "meditate" . Of course morning is ideal, because it can set the tone for the day. If you have to do it another time of day, that is alright too. Remember, the goal is to be consistent with your daily practice, so make it work for you. I often meditate at night, because I like the stillness of my house when everything has wound down for the day and I can ride that emerging quiet into a deep state.

3. Check in with how you're feeling. As you first settle into your meditation session, simply check to see how you're feeling. How does your body feel? What is the quality of your mind? Busy? Tired? Anxious? Whatever you're bringing to this meditation session as completely OK.

4. Become aware of your breathing. Now that you're settled in, turn your attention to your breath. Just focus on your breath as it comes in, and follow it through your nose all the way down to your lungs. Notice it as you exhale. Exhale long and deep, observe that quiet space that comes right after your exhale is finished, right before your next inhale. It sounds so simple, right? Focus on your breathing. Some people choose to focus their awareness on something else, a phrase you can repeat over and over in your mind, the gentle light of a candle burning, or some soothing sound or music.

5. Come back when you wander. It is certain your mind will wander. There's no problem with that. The mind is just trying to do its "perceived" job. When you notice your mind wandering, simply and gently return to your breath. Again and again. This is your meditation practice. For some of you it will be easier than others. Be patient. I mentioned before that I will actually say to my mind when it intrudes, "not now, I am meditating; come back later".

6. Develop a loving attitude. When you notice thoughts and feelings arising during meditation, as they will, look at them with a friendly attitude. See them as friends, not intruders or enemies. They are a part of you, though not all of you. It's just not the time to engage with them.

7. Don't worry that you're doing it wrong. You're not doing it wrong. There is no wrong way. You are giving yourself the gift of meditation. How great! With time and regular practice your meditation will become more and more peaceful.

8. Get to know yourself. A side benefit of practicing meditation is that you'll see how your mind works, how busy it wants to be, what it wants to engage in. Observe and bring yourself back to your breath, letting go of thoughts. Over and over, again and again, with love and patience for yourself. Later on in your day you can contemplate your experience, how your mind wants to engage you during meditation. By getting to know your mind it will become easier and easier to still your mind.

9. Really commit yourself. Don't just say, "Sure, I'll try this for a couple days." Really commit yourself to meditate every single day. In your mind, be locked in, for at least a month. I understand that finding time might be difficult some days. On those days take just 5 minutes to sit for meditation. You'll be so glad you did.

10. You can do it anywhere. If you're traveling or something comes up in the morning, you can do meditation in your office. In the park. During your commute. As you walk somewhere, (yes, there is such a thing as walking meditation). Sitting meditation is the best place to start, but in truth, you're practicing for this kind of mindfulness for your entire life.

11. Follow guided meditation. If it helps, you can try following guided meditations to start with. There is an abundance of resources available online for guided meditation.

12. Check in with friends. While I like meditating alone, you can do it with your spouse or child or a friend. For some of you it might even work to do it with your Loved One you are caring for. Or make a commitment with a friend to check in with each other every morning after meditation. Having that support might help you stick with it for longer.

13. Find a community. Even better, find a community of people who are meditating and join them. This might be a Zen or Tibetan community near you (for example); go and meditate with them. Or sit quietly in the pews of your church when you have some alone time. Find an online group (join our FaceBook page, start a discussion, ask your questions, share your support, encourage others.

14. Acknowledge yourself when you're done. Be grateful that you had this time to yourself, that you stuck with your commitment, that you took the time to get to know yourself and make friends with your mind. That's an amazing and beautiful use of time in your life. Time is so precious, use it wisely.

Meditation isn't always easy or even peaceful. I've certainly had very "busy" meditations, yet still it has truly amazing benefits! You can start today, and continue for the rest of your life.

While scientific evidence extolling the virtues of meditation exist in great abundance, I will not bore you with the studies involved. I will however, pique your interest by summarizing the benefits that have been proven and the brain research that has been rolling in steadily for a number of years now, with new studies coming out just about every week to illustrate some new benefit of meditation. Or, rather, some ancient benefit that is just now being confirmed!

Similar to the benefits in the chapter on Exercise, the practice of Meditation appears to have an extraordinary number of neurological benefit as well as psychological effects. In addition to the literal changes to the brain itself, Meditation helps relieve our subjective levels of anxiety and depression, improve attention, concentration, and overall psychological well-being.

In addition:

- Meditation helps preserve the aging brain
- Meditation reduces activity in the brain's "me center" – which is my favorite benefit, because this allows us to broaden our perspective from the contracted world of our troubles in order that we might be able to encompass a larger view of our lives with its myriad of possibilities for healing and growth.
- Its effects rival antidepressants for depression, anxiety – two of the most common "side effects" of caregiving are depression and anxiety, creating a perceived need to depend on mediation, which in turn have their own checklist of side effects, many of which are serious.
- Meditation may lead to volume changes in key areas of the brain
- Just a few days of meditation improves concentration and attention – Even Prozac doesn't work this fast!

Meditation is not a panacea, but there's certainly a lot of evidence that it may do phenomenal good for those who practice it regularly. And its benefits seem to be felt after a relatively short amount of practice. It's certainly worth a shot: creating a few minutes in the morning or evening (or both), rather than turning on your phone or going online, or watching television, see what happens if you try quieting down your mind, or at least paying attention to your thoughts and letting them go without reacting to them.

Just a few minutes of meditation a day will make a huge difference. Meditation can give back so much of what you, the caregiver, has lost. A sense of space, perspective, quiet time, creativity and peacefulness, all of which enhance your life and well being.

Strategy 3: Prayer

"It is better in prayer to have a heart without words than words without a heart." - Gandhi

While I don't shy away from controversy, I also recognize that this is not the forum to encourage it either. And what greater way to fan the flames of people's passions than to open a discussion about the nature of God? Needless to say, all of us have defined for ourselves what the very idea of God means or doesn't mean, and those ideas range from atheism, to monotheism to polytheism; from God as a Man to God as the Natural World. Honestly, to me, for our purposes, our definition matters little. What does matter is that we begin to recognize what we *do* identify with, because our highest purpose in life must be to live congruently with that.

If we live out of synchronicity with the callings of our spirit, we are destined to wrestle with discontent, to the degree that we are out of sync. No matter the Source of order in the world, I believe *most* people can recognize and trust an intelligence at work. The mere contemplation of the stages of life, from birth to death, informs us that life indeed works in an intelligent and orderly fashion, whether or not our mental ability is able to comprehend the mechanism for such order. The most atheistic among us can argue against a Universal Intelligence while his heart beats and his lungs respire, his neurons fire and his body metabolizes. If any among us were put in charge of the administration of such high level functioning, I dare say the system would fall into disarray very quickly.

I only suggest that we identify with Life; that we turn our attention away from the voice of doubt and fear and develop the ability to listen to our most authentic voice.

Some people might consider Prayer and Meditation the same or similar. I will let you define this for yourselves, but for me, Prayer means a communion with that voice within that wants nothing but the best for me. I personally am most attuned to it at certain times and in certain places. When I am in nature, I am particularly tuned in to the magical, sacred nuances of life, and I feel the freedom to ask questions, or just listen as instructions are given from within. Or sometimes, I will just have a conversation. Like Stevie Wonder said, "if you feel your life is hard, just go have a talk with God".

A caregivers greatest asset is being able to marshal the emotional strength when all evidence would suggest the well has run dry. When the very idea of placing one foot in front of the other seems like a Herculean task, the ability to persevere must be conjured from places that might actually appear separate from ourselves.

One of the most recurrent themes in literature and cinema is the idea of the protagonist, with all possibilities for a successful outcome of their quest extinguished, discovering within themselves the wellspring of courage and ability that propels them on to victory. The story is as old as Aesop. Fortunately, we all have this ability, and as caregivers, we will at some point, need to open up a supply line for emotional and spiritual reinforcements.

Prayer is so sweet in its appeal, because at its most basic, it is simply an invocation, when we can freely admit our frailty. For Prayer to be authentic, we must be able to recognize the limitation of our current circumstances and in so doing, we become vastly open to the possibilities that lie dormant deeper within ourselves. Prayer also asks something of us that is so essential to the process of growth during times of tribulation.

The act of praying requires that we be open to the presence of something greater than ourselves. It does not even necessarily ask that we believe in anything, just that we are "willing to be open" to the possibility. In that *willingness* there is great potency.

The very nature of Prayer asks us to suspend our efforts momentarily, just long enough to contemplate our place in the Universe. In fact the Hebrew word for prayer is Tefilah. It is derived from a root word meaning to judge oneself. This surprising word origin provides insight into the purpose of Jewish prayer. The most important part of any Jewish prayer, whether it be a prayer of petition, of thanksgiving, praise of God, or of confession, is the introspection it provides, the moment that we spend looking inside ourselves, seeing our role in the universe and our relationship to God. It is not even necessary to ask for anything in particular, since any true power greater than ourselves would certainly already suspect our predicament.

In the New Testament, Jesus said to his disciples:

"In praying, do not babble like the pagans, who think that they will be heard because of their many words.

Do not be like them. Your Father knows what you need before you ask him."

As a caregiver, I understand the feelings of helplessness, hopelessness and despair; and yet, I have also experienced the ascendency of courage, faith and understanding as they bubbled up through the thick fog of defeat. I freely admit that sometimes, these things feel way beyond my reach, but never have they failed to re-emerge when they were needed most.

Prayer keeps us mindful of the best within us and around us. It illuminates the act of caring for a Loved One with Alzheimer's as a sacred act, where the daily responsibilities become ministrations of Love. **Prayer reminds us that we can choose freely, that we are not alone in this struggle, and we can utilize the emotional challenges of a tragic illness as the crucible in which to forge a stronger, more resilient version of ourselves.**

A few months ago, I was having a particularly hard time dealing with Linda's decline. On that particular day I was heartbroken because Linda did not recognize her sister, who was visiting from out of town. I left the house for a drive and I found myself sobbing in a way that I have never cried before. I began screaming loudly, "I can't do this; it's too much for me to handle"! My mind was racing with thoughts of defeat, resentment and failure. I was filled to capacity, there was no room for light, or so it felt. Suddenly, from someplace within myself that seemed to be beyond the noise and suffering, I heard a voice speak clearly and authoritatively. It said "You are not alone, We will do this together". In that very moment, I felt all fear and resentment lift, replaced by a calm that was so deep it felt surreal. I was stunned into silence, and grateful for the experience although it took days before I could speak about it to anyone. It occurred to me that my state of absolute surrender was in itself a prayer. My tears were an offering that by some grace was received and responded to. I cannot say that experience was the beginning of daily revelations of such magnitude, but I can say, that my life did change in that moment. I continue to offer up my struggle and ask for strength, which is to say, I continue to pray. In a sense, my whole life has become a prayer that this experience, for me *and* for Linda, serves to evoke from us something of a higher order.

Prayer need not be articulate and eloquent, but earnest and sincere, as if the soul itself were crying out. As such, perhaps even a simple sigh can be thought of as a prayer. Many devout people pray in ways that circumvent the traditional notion of prayer. Encounters with God have occurred through song and silence, poetry and dance, tears and sighs. Such prayer may be what Paul describes in his letter to the Romans: "We do not know what we ought to pray for, but the Spirit himself intercedes for us through wordless groans" (Roman 8:26). Charles Spurgeon, the well known Baptist preacher tells us "groanings which cannot be uttered are often prayers which cannot be refused".

The Quakers, or the Society of Friends, focus much more on listening than on talking, on forming questions more than spouting answers. I recently read that 'they deliberate about important matters for their community by drafting "queries". In their meeting-houses, Quakers sit in silence and let these queries sink deep into their hearts. When they feel the Spirit move them to speak, only then do they rise, speak, and then continue in silence until someone else is moved by the Spirit. Their worship is overwhelmingly devoted to quiet inner listening, "waiting upon the Lord". After sitting with their queries, sometimes for years, Quakers make changes in their common life by consensus. Prayer opens the door to the vast expanse of spiritual fortitude necessary to grow and heal a caregiver.

- *Once a man was asked. "what did you gain by regularly praying to God?'*

'Nothing, but let me tell you what I lost: anger, ego, greed, depression, insecurity and fear of death. Sometimes, the answer to our prayers is not gaining, but losing; which ultimately is the gain."

I don't think about prayer in the conventional sense, yet, I feel a connection that I have a desire to explore. It is a yearning to connect; a desire to walk a path that is purposeful and valuable. With time, it becomes a way of being, as if the lessons of the struggle have taught me how fragile life can be, and as such, I want simply to distill the experience of life to its most poetic. Just like poetry can illuminate the truth with an economy of language, prayer can bring our desire for virtue to the forefront of our experience, and our lives will be better for it.

<u>Strategy 4: Contemplation/Journaling</u>

"No one can tell your story so tell it yourself. No one can write your story so write it yourself"

"If a story is in you, it has got to come out" -
William Faulkner

With all of this space cleared out and a yearning born of genuine desire to have the caregiving experience be a healing one, we now get to ask ourselves questions born of honesty and courage. For real…what kind of people do we want to be?

Let's stoke the fires of our imagination and have a conversation with ourselves about ourselves! What does it mean to be compassionate? Patient? Empathetic? Courageous? Inspiring? Loving? WHAT DOES IT TAKE?

I personally like to write, because it holds me more accountable to the dialogue inside of myself. Writing gives contemplation depth and footing. It makes it real. There have been so many times that I have gone back to see what I have written during my times of contemplation, to remember, who I am and who I want to be during a time when I feel perilously close to losing myself, because caregiving can suck the soul out of my marrow.

When you contemplate bad thoughts and bad impressions, your mind experiences corresponding states. I am quite certain you have had the experience of thinking negative thoughts and becoming full of negativity. So how long will it take for you to become full of optimism when you are thinking of new, expansive possibilities for a positive life?

In the first strategy, Eliminate the Negatives, I mentioned that some questions move us in the wrong direction, while others can elevate our thinking.

Questions like, 'why me?' do little to serve us, while there are other questions, when posed, that will allow us to follow their thread to greater understanding of what it means to be a healthy caregiver. Questions like, how do I maximize my health during such a stressful time? How, where and to whom can I reach out for support from people who have been through this and can guide me? What are my blocks to get through this time of caregiving for my Loved One so I can emerge healthier and at peace?

The poet, Rainer Maria Rilke, spoke of holding questions, living questions: *"Love the questions themselves…Don't search for the answers, which could not be given to you now, because you would not be able to live them. And the point is to live everything. Live the questions now. Perhaps then, someday far in the future, you will gradually, without even noticing it, live your way into the answer."*

In "Becoming Wise: An Inquiry into the Mystery and Art ", Krista Tippett says, *"we all have it in us to formulate questions that invite honesty, dignity, and revelation. There is something redemptive and life-giving about asking a better question…My only measure of the strength of a question now is in the honesty and eloquence it elicits. If I've learned nothing else, I've learned this: a question is a powerful thing, a mighty use of word"*.

I've always wondered about the fate of millions of inspired thoughts swirling above the heads of so many people, that will slip into oblivion, simply because time wasn't taken to write them down.

The art of Contemplation and Journaling is a wellspring for creativity, clarity, resolution and healing. It is a time we set aside to build the foundation of a new perspective out of existing circumstances.

While all of these strategies are written for us as caregivers, of course they have universal applicability. However, you and I are in a community of people who understand, tearfully at times, the enormous struggle of taking care of a Loved One with Alzheimer's Disease and other dementias. And we are painfully familiar with the toll it takes on us, especially emotionally. We must hold on to the idea that our lives can still be joyous and purposeful if we do the work necessary to allow us to grow and feel more connected to our humanity.

Caregiving is a rich tapestry of stories. It is a deeply personal story and it also incorporates the larger story of the community of caregivers. You know the feeling of immediate kinship and familiarity you feel when you find yourself in a conversation with another caregiver. Our stories, while extremely personal and intimate, are remarkably intertwined. At any support group for caregivers, there is always the unmistakable nodding of heads in a display of recognition of one's own story whenever someone else shares theirs. Stories are so vital to the creation of the narrative that brings us awareness and perspective!

Krista Tippett says, "*A story is all there, but we know that the story, the real story, is inarticulate. And I love that. I love the spaces in between what happens…Words make worlds…You have your own stories, the dramatic and more ordinary moments where what has gone wrong becomes an opening to more of yourself and part of your gift to the world. This is the beginning of wisdom…We are all healers of the world. That story opens a sense of possibility. It's not about healing the world by making a huge difference. It's about healing the world that touches you, that's around you."*

We put the strategies of Contemplation and Journaling together because they compliment each other so perfectly. Contemplation is the artful ability to observe and reflect on life's circumstances and your personal relationship to them, while Journaling or writing offers you the opportunity to give voice to your thoughts and feelings. It gives them legitimacy and value and makes them real. When we write, we find out what we didn't know we knew! We write to know deeper and truer. We write to connect the dots and create a whole new constellation of possibilities. In Contemplation, the pieces of ourselves and our circumstances become illuminated, and in Journaling we bring all the wayward parts of ourselves together, to discover more intimately who we are and what we are capable of.

Contemplation is not dwelling on the difficulties of your travails and replaying the endless loop of how burdensome your life has become. *Contemplation is giving deep consideration and reflection to where your heart is in relation to all that is going on around you.* It is paying attention to the voice within you that speaks from possibility, for it is never affected or diminished by circumstance.

Caregiving is a time when the weight of our thoughts can be crushing and it can be so difficult to lift ourselves above our circumstances. The copious and oppressive thoughts have a way of filling our mind and pushing out all of the free space available. It feels as if there is no space to create new ways of seeing, of being. Writing is a way to create a path of egress for all of those burdensome thoughts to outflow into the outer world, leaving precious room inside to reflect. In Eastern mysticism, it is said that God exists in the space between the in-breath and the out-breath; to which I will add that God exists in the space left behind when thoughts are cleared away.

So go ahead and fill pages and volumes with your stories as a caregiver. Write about your fears, your frustrations, your desires and your dreams. "*Fill your paper with the breathings of your heart*" said Wordsworth, because we write to make sense of the world.

If you want to improve your perspective on life and clarify issues, start writing in a journal, create a blog or write a book. When the distractions of daily life deplete our energy, the first thing we eliminate is the thing we need the most: quiet, reflective time. Time to dream, time to contemplate what's working and what's not, so that we can make changes for the better. Contemplation and Journaling bring clarity, accountability, self-awareness, reduce stress and allow you to freely vent. It also gives you peace of mind, allows you to track the progress of your personal growth, and perhaps above all, it is a safe place to just be yourself with no one judging.

It has been said that it's as easy as sitting down at the keyboard and putting one word after another until it's done. In my contemplations and writings, I always allow myself to go wherever the creative energy wants to take me. Sometimes it can take me to very dark places, indeed. While at other times, I am so pleased to see that possibility and optimism remain such a strong and essential part of my character. But I do not edit the process because I know, that caregiving has given me the opportunity to deal with the full spectrum of emotion available to me, and seeing it for what it is, allows me to shape it into something that will serve me in my personal growth. It also takes me way outside of where I would typically feel comfortable, which reveals and opens whole new parts of me to explore.

Some years ago, prior to Linda being diagnosed, I could not have imagined that the relative normalcy of my life would have morphed into having to hide the car keys from my wife, having to hand feed her and struggle to understand what she was trying to communicate.

I came across the following contemplation by Shannon Adler and immediately recognized it as a wonderful series of questions we could all benefit from in our evolution as people walking the caregiver's path:

"What if you were wrong? What if everything you ever believed was a lie? What if you missed your opportunity because you didn't know your worth? What if you settled on familiar, but God was trying to give you something better? What if you decided not to go backwards, but forward? What if doing what you have never done before was the answer to everything that didn't make sense? What if the answer wasn't to be found in words, but in action? What if you found the courage to do what you really wanted to do and doing it changed your whole life?"

Caregiving is the hurricane that reduces the familiar routine of our lives to rubble.

In Hamlet, Shakespeare said, *"Thinking makes it so."*

The lives of some caregivers will be condensed to the least common denominators of misery and suffering. Yet others will view it as the challenge of a lifetime and treat it like an Alchemist would, creating something of great value from something of lesser value..

Hemingway said, *"Writing is easy. Just sit down at a typewriter and bleed"*, to which he added, *"Write hard and clear about what hurts"*.

At a recent dinner, I had a conversation with a person I had met just that evening. We talked animatedly about change, and she told me that she loved change and that she welcomed it. Her husband looked at her with eyes wide open and reminded her that she detested change. That indeed, no one meets change kicking and screaming as much as she did. I confess, I found this conversation amusing and I told them as such. It occurred to me that there was a time that I would have thought the very same thing, that I welcome change. It only occurred to me after Linda's diagnosis that in fact, I have always been uncomfortable with change. I must have confused the small, inconsequential changes that happen routinely with *real change*. But when real change began to happen, I would have done anything to turn back the clock to B.C. (before change!).

It has only been through the process of deep contemplation over these very change filled years that I can now honestly say, I do enjoy change because it allows possibility and growth to flourish and dominate over stagnation. Isn't it ironic that change is what we fear most and it is exactly what is necessary to break us open to become the people we need to become to experience peace and contentment. Caregiving is all about change on so many levels. It creates a radical shift in the narrative of our lives and in the microcosm of things. Caregiving itself changes constantly as the illness progresses and we have to deal with our Loved Ones differently and more creatively, all the while looking for ways to better take care of ourselves.

Unless we engage in this process consciously, with the awareness cultivated from Contemplation, the changes will happen *to* us, instead of *from* us. We can discover why we cling to optimism despite the prevalence of the tenacious sway some of our negativities have over our lives. The only real reason to write is to find your voice; to discover yourself, hidden under the rubble that has accumulated over our lifetime.

A musician said, "I showed up to an empty page in a quiet room and asked my guitar, "what do I need to know?"

William Styron brilliantly wrote about his own depression in Darkness Visible, A Memoir of Madness, *"A second self—a wraithlike observer who, not sharing the dementia of his double, is able to watch with dispassionate curiosity as his companion struggles against the oncoming disaster, or decides to embrace it."*

A beautiful example of the contemplations and writings of someone searching for healing within their own illness.

"If you didn't write from a place of excruciating candor, you've written nothing". - Joni Mitchell

Contemplation and Journaling can also abbreviate suffering. Why do I assume that reams of pages filled with copious amounts of struggle are necessary? Perhaps one needs only to acknowledge suffering to move on. Thank it for being such a good teacher; even invite it to your graduation; but damn it, move on. Fill volumes with the celebration of what comes after suffering!

Strategy 5: Reading

"It is what you read when you don't have to that determines what you will be when you can't help it."
  - Oscar Wilde

The beautiful thing about reading is that there are countless people that have suffered as we have and much worse, who articulate their lessons in a way that can abbreviate our struggle. Why not, sit at the feet of the artists, poets, philosophers and scientists who have distilled the wisdom of countless ages into bite size lessons that can give us wings where before there was just a ball and chain?

Have you ever been asked the question, "who in all of history, do you wish you could sit and have a conversation with?" Of course, no one can answer that question for you, but doubtless your answer would be someone whose life was in some way an inspiration to yours. Perhaps a figure from the distant past, recent past, or even the present, whose attitude, actions, perspective or thinking has helped forge the best parts of your personality and left feeling hopeful and inspired.

Caregiving is a time in our lives when the very bonds that tether us to sense of self are frayed unimaginably. Outside our windows there seems to be a cultural wave of cynicism and fear that have taken a stronghold over so much of our thinking. It becomes increasingly difficult to distill the essential lessons of life from so much static and noise. Wouldn't it be empowering if we could cut through the distractions with the hard fought wisdom of centuries of great minds and hearts who have come before us and recorded their thoughts to speak to us for all time?

I have always loved to read. One of my fondest memories of childhood was passing by my parents bedroom and seeing my father with his nightlight on, reading into the evening. With his single bulb night lamp illuminating his book in the dark room, it had a reverential mystique to it. There was a feel to it that endures still, as I read into the evening hours.

It is very easy for me to fall prey to the dark voices of fear and resentment as I struggle with the challenges of helplessly watching Linda , as her Early Onset Alzheimer's carries her further and further away from me. So I call upon old friends, whose words fly off the pages and fill me with the wisdom culled from the challenges of their own lives.

I love to read things that are uplifting and inspiring and contribute to the journey that I am on. Many people have suffered so mercilessly and found the inner strength to persevere in a way that emboldened them to live extraordinary lives. So many men and women have had the courage and the rebelliousness to look at life differently than the rest of the world and share their vision for others to follow.

Thinkers and dreamers whose ideas have changed not just what we think but *how* we think, whose words can still be as close to us as our bedside table. *The very thought that we can stand in front of our bookshelves (or our Kindle!) and be in the presence of the greatest minds in history is almost incomprehensible.*

These days, I often turn to the stories of other individuals whose forbearance serves as an inspiration to me and reminds me that there is a community of people, past and present who understand *exactly* what it is like to face steep challenges, and have themselves, persevered. I can choose books to be inspired, uplifted, educated, or simply as an escape if I need a vacation from my life as a caregiver.

Reading is a conscious choice to turn off the noise of a collective voice that does not serve us on our path of growth and development at a time when that must be our primary focus. Reading is one more imperative in our vigilance so that our commitment to our growth and healing is unassailable.

Being a caregiver to a Loved One with Alzheimer's can occupy some of the best and potentially productive years of our lives. *To make a personal declaration that these years will be committed to discovering the highest attributes within ourselves not only serves us personally, but allows us to give extraordinary care to the ones we love.* Standing on the shoulders of other people whose struggles serve as a beacon to our own, grants us a perspective from which to learn and grow. I think the greatest ideal for a caregiver's life is to serve as an inspiration to other people as well as other caregivers, while taking care of your Loved One with an open heart, compassion and honor.

Immersion into the words of saints might not make us saints, but it can certainly make us more saintly! And imagine if we all had the resolve of Captain Ahab in Herman Melville's **Moby Dick,** when he says, *"Swerve me? ye cannot swerve me…The path to my fixed purpose is laid with iron rails, whereon my soul is grooved to run. Over unsounded gorges, through the rifled hearts of mountains, under torrents' beds, unerringly I rush! Naught's an obstacle, naught's an angle to the iron way!"*

There are books that teach us how to grieve, how to cope and even how to make sense of mortality. Literature can provide us with clarity, endurance, faith and humor. Yes humor! Let's not forget to laugh. Laughter in itself is healing and relieves stress. The words of great writers can help us to articulate our own fears, hopes and desires, all necessary in the process of healing as caregivers.

The words of great and even ordinary men and women who have had the courage to contemplate life's challenges, forging meaningful and impactful ways to address them successfully, have left a trail for us to follow. Get under your covers, turn on the nightlight, pick a book that moves you, and open your heart and mind to new possibilities.

Strategy 6: Exercise

Be Stronger Than Your Excuses

Illness and disease are often the result of the body's inability to adapt successfully to stress. Whether it is a physical, chemical or emotional stress, if the body cannot adapt, illness is the result. The body must be able to adapt to stress or it will deteriorate disproportionately. There are few things proven to counter the ravages of stress and afford the body the ability to adapt as well as Exercise and Eating Well. And there are few things that are more accessible to every caregiver. Part of the appeal of these strategies for healthy caregiving is there availability. Each of them, including Exercise can be done with just a modicum of time, energy and commitment.

Taking walks, which you can do with your Loved One, stretching while watching TV, a simple routine at home or making a commitment to work out at a gym for 45 minutes a few days a week, if that is possible, will all work quite well. My personal favorite is taking walks and hikes. I used to love going on hikes with Linda when she was still able. She became calmer and enchanted when we were in a beautiful place and were getting exercise. And of course, since hiking together was something we had always loved to do, it brought us back to the comfort of the familiar. It was a time of sweetness and simplicity with little else to distract us.

It is likely that for a caregiver, regular exercise becomes one of the first casualties. Obviously, there are the time constraints that seem to impose themselves on every spare tick of the clock. And of course there are the reserves of energy whose depletion quickly reach drought proportions. I have always exercised regularly and I know as well as any caregiver the frustration of that closing window of opportunity. Time set aside during the week for exercise, is usually stolen by something else, frustratingly, almost always related to caregiving. Exercise, is literally about putting one foot in front of the other, a spot on metaphor for caregiving, which in itself, is often just about putting one foot in front of the other, and we know how difficult that can be for many of us at times. At my worst moments as a caregiver, when I thought the idea of a joyful future was nothing more than an empty wish, people would ask me how I was doing, and my response was "I'm putting one foot in front of the other." Looking back, that response, the act of literally putting one foot in front of the other was just too rooted in the negative. Not to mention that I was exhausted and I simply could not marshal the forces necessary to make it happen.

Most of the others strategies are psycho-spiritual, but exercise is a devoutly physical act, with beneficial psycho-spiritual side effects. *You actually must get off your butt to make it happen, even in the face of time constraints and exhaustion.* **Especially for the caregiver of a Loved One with Alzheimer's disease, the benefits of Exercise are at the very least, extremely beneficial and at best, nothing short of transformational in creating a better and more balanced life.**

During the middle years of my caregiving experience, there was a long dry spell, where I watched myself lose all of the benefits gained from my regular exercise routine. I felt terrible as a result, and my caregiving experience descended into the hellish abyss of chronic fatigue, depression and bouts of depression. All because I was leaving out one of the most important ingredients of a healthy life. It happened more in the middle years because early on, I was obviously still able to leave Linda by herself when I went to the gym. As time progressed and it became clear that leaving her alone was no longer an option, we would take long walks and hikes together, so exercise was still a regular part of the routine, which was great for both of us. As time passed it became more difficult to hike with her because she developed the tendency to saunter off trail and I was afraid of her getting lost. When I tried to coax her back to the trail, she would often get angry, while my rosy temperament was being strained at the seams. So it became just too difficult to hike together and make the time for other exercise, and that is when I fell into a long exercise drought. My well being suffered noticeably. My fitness waned, I put on weight, my mental acuity became blurred. Worst of all, the energy to just be involved in the the particulars of life diminished greatly.

Movement is Life and that can be taken as a truism at any level. For life to prosper, a body must stay in motion, a mind must be flexible and the human spirit must remain active and engaged. Life does not favor the static.

Sometimes I have moments of epiphany, when the sum total of my experience is overwhelmed by the desire to transcend my current circumstance and I can no longer accept the behaviors and habits that have not been serving me. In such a moment, it feels like a switch has flipped inside me and my mind immediately embraces a new possibility. I am aware of the efforts involved, but the rewards now far outweigh the complacency.

I mentioned previously that my favorite exercise is hiking, and I love when it is strenuous. I feel most whole when I am in nature and to engage it in such a way will always bring me back to the version of myself that feels the best. Exercise is self perpetuating, what some might even call a healthy addiction, because after all, who doesn't want to feel great? For me, hiking also embraces several of the 9 Strategies, ME Time, Contemplation, Prayer and it can even be considered meditative. Especially for caregivers, who experience such burdensome drains on their physical and emotional resources, when they are given the opportunity to feel a genuine lightening of the gravity of their stress, it can be intoxicating.

What a radical and uplifting shift, when people ask me how I am doing and I can now tell them how good I feel. I can climb a set of stairs without being out of breath, my pants fit and my overall state of mind is much improved!

The implication is not that caregiving has gotten easier, or the tragic decline of my beautiful wife is something that I now have become comfortable with, because that is not the case. However, the difference is that now there is an ease in my ability to deal with the worst of it. Now there is a real experience that in the presence of my challenges there is a strength and elasticity that make everything feel so...do-able.

I have learned through Linda's illness that life can throw curve balls that we never see coming. I have come to appreciate that there is so much out of my control. While at the same time, we learn to do what we can with what has been given to us.

We do have some control over the day to day nurturing of our body. Our body is the physical home that we get to have this distinctly human experience in for as long as we are here on this earth. If we wear it out, where are we going to live?

In Thoreau's "Walking", he reminds us of how the simple act of sauntering, connects us with an essential part of ourselves, a certain vitality that all too commonly gets lost in the routine of our sedentary lives, proclaiming that "*every walk is a sort of crusade.*" Thoreau is careful to point out that the walking he extols has nothing to do with transportational utility or physical exercise — rather it is a spiritual endeavor undertaken for its own sake. While written with sincerity, I cannot help finding a certain whimsy in this. While as a walker, I can attest to the spiritual benefits of walking through the woods, I also know that you can get a whole lot of exercise!

Multiple studies have verified the profound impact, not just on our physiology, but our mental and emotional states as well. I came across a website called, thebrainflux.com, which is a compendium of contemporary research on brain function, self described as "The latest information straight from research and experts on how to improve your brain, behavior, and performance." I found so much of the information on exercise compelling enough to list a handful of proven benefits.

The cognitive benefits of exercise include:

1. Improving your executive functions or your higher level thinking skills. Even if you're a little bit older, exercise can   improve these important cognitive skills

2. Increasing your IQ: Most people will tell you that exercising is a smart thing to do. But that's because it can literally make you smarter

3. Increasing your focus which means developing the skills to ignore distractions and concentrate on the task at hand

4. Increasing your cognitive flexibility which correlates with increases in mental speed, attention, and the ability to multitask

5. Increasing willpower, a key ingredient in successful caregiving to avoid becoming discouraged and to stay on track in taking care of ourselves and adhering to healthy habits

6. Helps to control emotions, such as allowing you to reign in an outburst of anger, or continue your day despite feelings of sadness. This fosters a decrease in emotional stress and an increase in emotional control. If you have a tendency to blow up at people or lose your calm, exercise can help you keep centered. Life is going to throw you a curveball or two, and a calm mind can help you navigate turbulent waters

7. Sharpens short term and long term memory

8. Allows us to think faster which makes it easier to be decisive and arrive at solutions and solving problems faster. And the results found did this across all ages

You can't talk about the brain without talking about psychology. Our moods, personalities, and motivations are what make us mentally unique. There are a number of things that can occur throughout the day that can affect our mental state. It's constantly changing, and life is going to give you a fair share of stressful situations. **Exercise has the ability to restore positive feelings, make you resilient to stressful situations, and might even increase your happiness levels**

The psychological benefits of exercise include:
1. Exercise alleviates stress and has a calming effect on a stressed mind

making it perhaps one of the most efficient stress management techniques

2. Gives you emotional resilience providing exercisers yet another level of protection from the day to day stress that happens to all of us

3. Reduces anxiety

4. Increases pain tolerance

5. Prevents and helps fight depression. Depression is one of the most common mental conditions that affects people worldwide, with caregivers particularly susceptible. Exercise produced positive results for relief from depression and was found to be just as effective as the other alternatives commonly used to combat depression

6. Improves your mood because exercise causes the release of feel good chemicals in the brain. If you're curious: the methods coming in   second and third were music and social interaction

7. Improves self-esteem which is important if we want to live a happy life. Low self esteem creates stress, depression, and anxiety. If gone unchecked it can also cause a number of other unhealthy behaviors. Exercise has been shown to affect self-esteem positively in all ages, from your development as a child right up into your senior years

8. Improves your quality of sleep

9. Helps you eat healthier

10. Increases your productivity

11. Protects against a sedentary lifestyle

12. Boosts creativity

In addition to the list above, there are a host of neurobiological benefits of exercise including increased energy, reduced fatigue and the slowing down of brain atrophy. **It is really quite astounding how far reaching the beneficial effects of exercise are for the caregiver.** As the most complex organ in the body, it got us to where we are today, and who knows where it can take us in the future

It bears repeating: movement is life, and movement infiltrates every aspect of our being. **Exercise keeps us engaged and focused on the goal of becoming healthy and staying healthy. It locks us into purposeful living which is the antidote to the depressive spiral which so often affects the caregiver. I know this downward spiral intimately as I know the saving grace in seizing control of my circumstances by making healthy choices. Take a walk, see the world for the first time with the eyes of possibility**

Strategy 7: Eating Well

Note to Myself: When I Eat Like Crap, I Feel Like Crap

Can anything be more true than the saying you are what you eat? If you put foods into your body that nurture healthy, living cells and tissue, you will promote your health. Despite the glut of books on the market about all the fad diets, the basics of good nutrition are ridiculously simple. By eliminating certain foods, the body has a wondrous capacity to regenerate itself, and the mind returns to clarity. Even our emotions will begin to even out when we are Eating Well.

Ok, so here goes my testimonial, but my confession first.

I have been a chiropractor for over three decades, and one of my core responsibilities is to encourage and inspire people to make healthy choices. Obviously, one of the more accessible choices that people can make has to do with Eating Well. It is relatively easy; there is information about proper nutrition everywhere you turn; it requires no more effort than eating poorly, and in fact might even be less expensive, on your wallet and ultimately your overall health. No one would ever doubt that the rewards of Eating Well are huge. So why would anyone choose to eat poorly?

When Linda's illness became overwhelming for me, one of the very first casualties was my commitment to eat well. For the first two years following her diagnosis, I ordained myself the family chef/nutritionist and placed both of us on an immaculate program of optimal nutrition in the expectation that Linda's illness somehow had a metabolic cause and we would find some resolution in healthy eating. Two years later, Linda's condition had deteriorated dramatically as did her body weight, to the point where it became alarming. She started at a beautiful 150 pounds and shrank down to a frightening 107 pounds. I abandoned the pristine eating regime and we both agreed she should just eat whatever she wanted to try to gain back some of the weight. She continued to lose weight dramatically, despite the fact she was eating whatever she wanted. Linda could put it away with the best of them!

But...back to my confession.

There came a point where the progression of her illness was accelerating and I was having trouble keeping up with it emotionally. I began to sink into all of the negative emotions that most caregivers travel through, and that resulted in a giving up of sorts. I stopped exercising as regularly as I had, and I traded Eating Well for eating conveniently. I was just to fried (pun intended!) to devote much energy at the end of the day to preparing healthy meals, or even to plan ahead, which would have been so much easier. My weight ballooned from 205 to 232 pounds, and my level of energy sank to an all time low. The poor quality of foods I was eating was contributing to everything from depression to feelings of failure and low self esteem. What a conundrum! Here I was having to take care of the woman I love at a time when she needs me the most, and I could barely take care of myself. I could probably have bought a small country house just with the money I wasted on terrible take out food! But...it was easy and I was tired and cranky. So ends my confession. In a nutshell, I dropped the ball by making poor eating choices and I paid a dear price for it.

And now for my testimonial...

The inevitable shift in the process was when I became sick and tired of feeling sick and tired. Not only was I heavier than I had ever been, and I was taking care of Linda in a way that was quite unfair to her. She needed my attentiveness and all I could offer her was my fatigue. I began to feel like the best years of my life were slipping away because I felt so poorly. I know it's odd to define caregiving as the best years of my life, and yet somehow I feel as if they have been the most spiritually transformational and have taught me the most valuable lessons about life.

At some point, a switch flipped inside of me and the calling to get back to being healthy seemed like the obvious choice and I erased all other options. I simply got sick and tired of feeling sick and tired. **I know how to eat well, I just misplaced the ability to care enough to make it happen.** So in the span of a couple of weeks, I eased myself into eliminating the foods that I knew were harmful to me physically, emotionally and even psychologically. As I did, I replaced them with foods that were highly nutritious, lighter, and contributed to the state I was looking to achieve. **Within days of beginning, miraculously (not really, because anyone can experience the exact same results!), I began to think more clearly, feel way more comfortable in my body and most importantly, my mood had begun to transform. I was feeling happier again!** And with that, the ability to take care of Linda improved, my bounce came back at the office and I simply began to feel the way I know I am supposed to feel when I take care of myself. On a selfish note, the thought had crossed my mind more than once, that I wanted to make sure, if Linda should pass before I do with her illness so advanced, that I was still healthy so I could continue to participate in life at the level that I enjoy. I honestly believe that I owe that not just to myself, but to my lovely wife who has always wanted only the best for me.

It really is a very simple equation: if we fill our bodies with lifeless food where all of the nutrition has been processed out of them, we will end up just as lifeless, with the best parts of ourselves processed out as well. However, if we nourish ourselves with food that is rich in life and nutrients, all of the laws of nature conspire in our favor and we become much better versions of ourselves. As we often talk about, the caregiving years of our lives are some of the most stressful we will ever experience. For a person to remain healthy (and disease free, I might add), their bodies must be able to adapt as successfully as possible to the duress it must endure. **A body that is well nourished is highly more adaptable to stress and thus far more capable of maintaining itself.**

Would you think about strewing trash around your house and wading through mounds of filth? Would you pour sugar into your gas tank? **Our bodies quite literally are our homes while we reside in this earthly realm, so doesn't it serve us to the highest ends to take impeccable care of our bodies? If you wear out your body, where are you going to live?**

We have an opportunity as caregivers to learn the lessons in life that will bring out the best in us. Caregiving is in itself one huge opportunity to figure out what it means to live an extraordinary life under the most challenging of circumstances. All great journeys begin at home. **Home is your body; your body is in your sacred trust; take care of it and show it the respect and love it deserves! The worst that can happen is your life will be greater for it.**

Strategy 8: ME Time

"There is a difference between loneliness and solitude, one will empty you and one will fill you"
- AVA

It is widely accepted that one of the single most difficult decisions for a caregiver to make, is to allow someone else to assume some of the responsibilities of caring for their Loved One. Whether it is a friend, family member or professional, the very idea of having someone do what you think you alone are qualified for, is heart wrenching.

It is not as if you don't know you need relief. You crave it, like a starving man craves a T-bone steak. Every cell in your being is screaming for time apart from the most stressful circumstance you have ever had to endure, and yet…so many questions present roadblocks. For me the questions were: can anyone else possibly know Linda's wants and needs more than I do? What if I am not there and she is upset and in need of consolation? Who can console her better than me? How could she ever be as comfortable with anyone else but me?

Despite the urgings of my close and supportive friends to bring in professional help, I adamantly held the line with a very resolute NO. My wife is my responsibility. My friends saw me losing traction down the slippery slope of exhaustion, burnout, physical deterioration and financial stress from not being able to focus on my business. They comforted me through buckets of tears and leaden eyelids. They saw a man on the verge of losing it. And through it all, I fixated on the one statistic that frightened me the most; that over 60% of caregivers will die before their Loved Ones, because of the immense stresses involved.

I knew two things: I didn't want to die and I didn't want Linda to be without me. So, the only reasonable solution was that I had to take better care of myself, which was impossible until I allowed myself some time away from being a caregiver 24/7. With great reluctance, even outright resistance, I acquiesced to the appeals of those who knew me best and I began to interview professional caregivers. After five or six interviews, I finally found someone who inspired enough confidence in me to give it a try. And the pivotal point in the interview that assured me, was not her clinical skills or her experience, it was that she cried when I told her how much my wife meant to me and that I wanted her to feel respected and loved. When I saw her tears, something inside me clicked, and I knew I was entering a new possibility.

This is the part of the story where you cue the celestial trumpets and singing angels, because when I had my first hours away from taking care of Linda, I felt like I had just ran through the gates of a prison into the arms of freedom. I felt liberated, not because I was away from my wife, but because now I knew that at least I could be away for restorative time, Me Time.

I also wanted to travel for a few days to visit family. Everything inside of me screamed "it's not possible". I couldn't imagine myself taking that much time away from Linda. It was Joko who strongly invited and encouraged me to be open to the possibility that it could work. Joko didn't stop there. She urged me to go away for a 2-night weekend and offered to stay with Linda. After much encouragement, and definitely not entirely at ease, I did. And guess what? Linda and Joko had a blast and I got to spend much needed time with my brother. WOW!

Those first few times were tentative at best, but it got easier until it became completely natural. And ironically, the great lesson is that the aides that have cared for Linda over time, do a far better job than I did in managing the day to day circumstances of this illness; and they do it with more professionalism, experience and confidence.

I gradually honed my usage of Me Time to where I felt refreshed and productive. I did the things I needed to do and the things I love to do. I wrote, read, visited with friends, exercised, went to movies, took hikes, handled business matters, whatever was asking to be done. I became infinitely more relaxed. More than anything, time away opened up the space inside my consciousness, which allowed me to broaden my perspective of this whole scenario.

When I was in the middle of it, deep fried and fat, caregiving occupied the totality of the available energy I had, in essence narrowing my vision to where caregiving became all that I was able to see. Freeing up space allowed me to sit further back in my theater, so I could take in more of the available screen of my life.

I provided care to my beautiful wife Linda when she lived at home. I did so with love and empathy and found joy in making her feel safe and comfortable. However, being a caregiver is not the sum total of who I am or what my life is about. Life is far too big to be locked into a closet and think that it contains the whole universe.

Rest is the only time your body has to recuperate and rebuild. Rest is getting the amount of sleep that you need, but it is also about finding time for yourself. It becomes imperative to create Me Time, time to be alone, to do the things that nurture and inspire you. It can be as simple as taking a walk, reading a book, or using that time to be with your friends for an evening of fun and conversation. Go stand in front of great works of art, listen to music that moves your soul, whether it's Beethoven or the Allman Brothers. Turn off the television from time to time. **Time for yourself creates perspective and revitalization.**

"The man who fears to be alone will never be anything but lonely, no matter how much he may surround himself with people. But the man who learns, in solitude and recollection, to be at peace with his own loneliness, and to prefer its reality to the illusion of merely natural companionship, comes to know the invisible companionship of God. Such a one is alone with God in all places, and he alone truly enjoys the companionship of other men…"
— Thomas Merton, No Man Is an Island

I went out the other evening to see a movie and have some dinner. At that point Linda was needing to be in a nursing home, because the demands of her illness had outpaced my abilities to take care of her. I used to love doing that alone, even when Linda was well. Having some time to myself always felt sublime. It was about 9:30 pm, I was at the restaurant and I didn't have anyone waiting for me at home. I had no pressing early appointments the next day, yet still, I had this clawing discomfort that I was supposed to get home. It was getting late and somehow I felt that I was needed at home. I had gotten so used to not having any time available alone, that I discovered, I had forgotten how to be alone in certain circumstances. It also seemed as if the punishments of my youth, like going to bed early and staying home on weekends had become the goals of my adulthood.

My life had become a box that I was uncomfortable living outside of. Yet, I was having such a sweet time. I was relaxed; I enjoyed the movie; I even met a great couple at the restaurant with whom I was engaged in lively and stimulating conversation. Finally, I just gave myself permission to relax into the evening and enjoy my time and all of a sudden joy flooded back into me. I made a promise to myself that I will start going to concerts, plays, films, even if it means staying out later than I had become accustomed to. It felt so good to stretch out.

Much has been written about the therapeutic value of alone time. I recently read Henry David Thoreau's book called Walking, in which he extols the virtues of spending hours everyday just sauntering through the woods near his home. It would be a time where he would leave his cares behind and immerse himself in the majesty and the grandeur of the forest, identifying with the higher aspects of his own nature.

If there is one strategy that I would implore you to adopt, it would be this one, Me Time. Become open to the fact that you must carve some restorative time out of your day. **It is with Me Time that many of the other strategies can take root. Whether it is meditation, reading, writing or exercising, find, in any way you can, the time for yourself.** Do nothing, lay in the grass and look at the leaves swaying in the wind, or do something that makes you want to walk down the sidewalk with a bounce in your step and a glimmer of hope. Change it up! Step outside your box. Try it, you will be so glad you did.

Time is the currency that pumps life into my dreams. With Me Time, I can sculpt and mold a future with all of its alluring possibilities. Everyone has dreams of a bright future but only a few corral the courage to actively work on their dreams so they can become a reality. As long as I have time to dream, I have time to create. Take that away from me and I face extinction. Take time from me and I have no currency left with which to imagine and change my life.

Imagine. A. Life.

As a caregiver, you learn to live outside of your needs often, dealing with your Loved One, other people, and their emotions. Putting your needs aside is a convenient adaptive mechanism and an 'easy' way to survive. There is so much that needs to be done "for" other people that it leaves precious little time to process your own emotions. The upside is you only have to deal with the surface of things in your own life; the downside is that you become a torrent of anger and frustration, with all of its tributaries and confluences, heading speedily towards a roiling boil. As such, I learned how *not* to live in the present. I squandered the present to create a future that I could live in. Looking back that just doesn't make any sense. Isn't that the great universal point that we all miss collectively? We save up our today's until we have enough of them to redeem for a prize sometime in the future? Imagine the desperation then, when you have to pay the caregivers tax, which is the mind numbing fee of the totality of your available time.

We've all been told endlessly of the value of living in the moment, but have never been taught the secret of how to do so. So now, when the moment, when your time, no longer belongs to you, it becomes even more complicated, for what is the appeal of living in someone else's moment?

Caregiving snaps us into the moment because we must process and deal with what is in front of us. With awareness, we can bring the lessons of the moment forward in creating a future for ourselves where the moments carry the seeds of their own contentment. Do not be afraid of getting your hands dirty. Do not shy away from the hard stuff. Take a swan dive into the deep end of the pool and come out stronger for it.

A few thoughts on "ME Time":
- *"The quieter you can become, the more you can hear"* - Ram Dass
- *"How can you hear your soul if everyone is talking"* - Mary Russell
- *"Solitude is the place of purification"* - Martin Buber
- *"Solitude, whether endured or embraced, is a necessary gateway to original thought"* - Jane Hirshfield
- *"In solitude there is healing. Speak to your soul. Listen to your heart. Sometimes in the absence of noise we find the answers"* - Dodinsky

When I finally embraced the fact that I cannot do without spending time away from Linda, or more specifically, away from the agonizing reality of the circumstances of her illness, something inside of me shifted. By giving myself the time necessary for my own process, I found myself more patient, kinder and far more available as her husband and caregiver.

"Loneliness is the poverty of the self; solitude is the richness of the self" - May Sarton
Sometimes solitude is one of the most beautiful things on earth...

Strategy 9: Living a Passionate Life

Every Next Level of Your Life Will Demand A Different You!

While it's always great to live in the "now" and "be in the moment," sometimes you need to look ahead to see where you want to go. If you don't change your direction, you're going to end up where the train is headed. Even if you end up in a another car on the same train, that *feels* different, you will still end up where the train is headed.

Living with a commitment to see things through the eyes of possibility is a shift that must be real and fundamental. Disassemble and reassemble yourself if you need to. Give birth to the next version of yourself, which is necessary if we want to remain healthy and vital. But make no mistake, caregiving is so difficult, that it requires nothing less; nothing less than the total investment of yourself.

Create distinctions for your life that make caregiving an opportunity for healing. **Create a vision for your life that is so compelling and inspiring, you will do whatever is necessary to make it happen.** Become an inspiration to your family, to your community, and even to your self; not by what you say, but by what you do and the good choices you make, creating a healthy future for yourself. Lead with love and compassion with your afflicted Loved One and have that love and compassion spill over into every aspect of your life. As Joko always says, *"take the journey from worrier to warrior!"*

When all's said and done, a caregiver's life is often something apart from the lives of the people who sit next to you on the bus, who work beside you, who you meet in the grocery store. It is not that your life is more difficult, or that other people don't have challenges of their own. It simply is that our burden is a *composite*, the sum total of the physical, emotional, spiritual, financial, familial stresses that are involved in taking care of a Loved One with Alzheimer's

Disease. It is a *compound* challenge, affecting almost every nook and cranny of our lives. One jagged arm of this multi-tentacled mess is reaching into your finances, while another is clutching at your heart, another is tearing your family asunder, while still more are wreaking havoc with your physical well being and your spiritual faith.

I honestly don't know if there will ever be a point where clarity will rise from the ashes of our struggle and we will one day understand the meaning of what we have had to endure. However, I do know that being happy is not about finding the answers to life. Even for the most spiritual among us, life will always have an element of mystery and that shouldn't frighten us, but intrigue and excite us. When we can accept that, we can begin to relax into the circumstances of our life. We can even discover that as we get older, the circumstances that used to confine us can begin to liberate us by reminding us how resilient we are. After all, despite the trials and tribulations of our lives, we are still here, aren't we?

Caregiving provides us with an opportunity to embrace the challenges of life and awakens us to the very possibility that we are bigger and better than we had ever imagined. **We are stronger, more durable and more capable. Yes, we are still fragile, but we are learning that our fragility is the door to our humanity through which we can feel more deeply the richness of life.** I don't believe that we are really searching for answers to life's questions at all. In fact, I don't even think we would know what to do with them if we found them. I believe what we are truly seeking is simply the *experience of being alive.*

People search for purpose and meaning in the mundane, which is why it is so easy to get lost in the never ending quest for more. But true passion comes from waking out of a torpor, and seeing our lives as something new. **Passion is seeing your life as a blank canvas while every instinct within you is compelling you, driving you, to create something of value.**

As caregivers, we are virtually thrown into the melting pot to have our lives forged and hammered until we become better versions of ourselves. We are practically given a paint by the numbers kit: apply some empathy here, courage here, understanding here, courage here, until we have unveiled the masterpiece of our life.

Don't we owe it to ourselves and our Loved Ones to become passionate about having a great life! It is only when we lose ourselves in service, that we can begin to find ourselves. That is when we can awaken the sleeping giant within. Imagine the quiet joy you feel when you witness your life becoming an inspiration to others and your ego doesn't get involved because you have learned that you have tapped into something that is available to all. Imagine the joy you feel when you lay your head on your pillow after a long day and you are able to say to yourself: "I did good today"

There is little about caregiving that is easy. It certainly is not for the meek. However the majority of people have reserves that they are not even aware of until they are called upon. And it is during these moments, when a person learns to becomes humble and obedient to the will of that yearning, or calling within himself, he is awakened. Awakened to a life where one can give and love and serve, not out of limitation and lack, but out of abundance as there is never a shortage of love.

When your commitment to having your life's journey is to be passionate and extraordinary, obstacles become mere speed bumps. Similarly, **when you know that life can be one damn thing after another, but you choose to persevere, you know that you have become unstoppable.**

Every single day, I wake up and within seconds I remember that I am living in the greatest challenge I have ever faced. And every single day, in that very moment, I am faced with a choice How can I live a life *today*, that is congruent with the calling of my spirit? How can I take care of my beautiful wife Linda, in a way that she continues to feel loved and safe? How can I *be* today, so when I lie in the darkness tonight, I can rest with a sense of tranquility and realize that I am transcending my challenges and embracing my life the way I know it should be lived? Do I succeed every day? Of course not! But I can say with a true and peaceful heart, that caregiving has and continues to give me the opportunity to Live a Passionate, Purposeful and Meaningful Life. And because of that, I *experience being alive.*

Conclusion

"A long view of time can replenish our sense of ourselves and the world." - Krista Tippett

I do not wish for anything I presented in these 9 Strategies to imply that this process is easy. Far from it. Every victory was hard fought for and won by a trail of heartaches, sorrows and tears. This is not meant to be a feel-good book. This is a do-something book. It does not ask the question of how do I survive caregiving, but rather how do I embrace caregiving in a way that my life is actually enhanced by having gone through it?

The Final Chapter doesn't end with the death of your Loved One. **The Final Chapter seeks resolution as the decisions that you've made about your life along this journey begin to bear fruit in a way that brings you contentment, satisfaction and peace.** Everything that comes before is a part of your story, a part of the narrative. This is not a journey of endurance, but one of healing, full of personal revelation, realizations, contemplations and understanding of our own frailties and strengths.

Our inspiration to create these 9 Strategies for caregivers occurred when someone who attended one of my talks a while back, mentioned that since becoming a caregiver, she approached her life with the question:

"What if…?"

In that moment, I thought it was so simple, yet so brilliant. 'What if we gave ourselves the attention we deserved, physically, emotionally and spiritually?' And even narrowed down, 'What if we ate well, just for one month?' 'What if we spent 15 minutes meditating just for today?' **An entire universe becomes possible, built on the shoulders of that simple question; each "what if…" tearing down a potentially ruinous set of circumstances and replacing**

them with a transformative experience.

What if…our experience of caregiving could be a shining example to other caregivers who struggle? What if…caregiving shifted from a fight for survival to an ongoing exercise in self love and love for others? Imagine the transformative effect on your consciousness, your health, your life, and our sphere of influence.
What if… you were committed to the evolution of caregiving as a process, ushering in a whole new paradigm in the caregiving community?

In this moment, my lovely wife, whom I adore, is in hospice care. She has lost her ability to swallow, her life is rapidly coming to an end. My heart is filled with sadness and at the same time, I am oddly at peace…oddly because this tranquility exists in the midst of great emotional upheaval…because I have looked for it, I have asked for it, I have meditated on it, contemplated it, read about it, wrote about it, prayed for it and nourished my body to receive it. If you search for something in earnest and are open to it…it will reveal its secrets.
Despair carries the seeds of transformation because it grinds us to our knees where we kneel prostrate before our own longing hearts. Kneeling in a puddle of our own tears, we learn to swim.

There must be a point when something extraordinary happens. Either a slow, deliberate process of growth, or moments of revelation, but the results somehow make your life better for having been through the tribulations. You can take your mind back from the enemies of fear and doubt; declare your mind off limits to the forces of darkness; drown out the fires of suffering with the cool waters of faith in a fulfilling future. Fix your mind on possibility and allow it to be the beacon of light that draws you forward, despite exhaustion, doubt and discouragement. My sadness is mourning for things lost; my faith is for the promise of greater things found as I cultivate faith and ask for wisdom and understanding. I will continue to listen for the voice.

In writing this book, I confess, I am eminently unqualified to speculate and postulate, however, by necessity, I have anointed myself with the expertise to do so! Many ideas contained in the 9 Strategies have been gleaned from what has come before. When such is the case, credit has been attributed. Our purpose is to bring to bear whatever information is germane to the basic premise of caregiving as an opportunity for growth and healing. The wisdom of healing has its genesis over eons, across continents, and can be found on cave walls, sacred scrolls, science texts, poetry and prose. My own ideas can be nothing but a stylistic synthesis of my experience which is hardly anything new, as loss is as old as time.

* * *

We have bought into the idea of despair and desperation with the sum total of our resources. What if...like a good financial consultant, we shifted our investments where there was a guarantee of greater returns? As I sit here with the clock ticking furiously fast on Linda's last moments, I am taking a moment to reflect on the 9 Strategies. Truth be told, I feel momentously out of sorts, which might just be a prideful phrase for depressed. In some ways, I still wrestle with failure: could I have done a better job taking care of my wife? Should I have kept her home? Should I have sat continuously at her bedside these last few weeks to serve as a constant reminder that she will never be alone until that moment when she must take her journey? Whether consciously or subconsciously, the anticipation of her passing and even her present suffering occupies the crevices of my brain like a thin autumnal morning mist, and it has settled itself so completely, it never leaves. Ever. If I am not thinking about it, I am feeling it. I am wearing it draped over my shoulders like a shawl. I don't know what to do with myself; I am crawling out of my skin and I want to scream to no one in particular. I want to stay in bed. I want to run away.

However...I don't. This morning I meditated deeply and swam around in a sea of sadness. Oddly, I felt grateful to discover that it's okay to be sad. My wife is about to die. My wife is, and has been the great love of my life. My one true love, if you would indulge me the syrupy sentiment. We were supposed to grow old together, take motorcycle trips, dance and laugh until we were too feeble to go on. We would die together, many years from now, holding hands and feeling sated. That was the plan. Instead, I am sitting at my computer, sharing my sadness, and wondering what will come next.

So... do these strategies make a difference or are they simply diversions meant to appease? Are our minds so wired for survival that we will create any reality to replace the one that doesn't feel good? I think back to the countless times that people have asked me how I am holding up. I have always replied with some version of "I feel peaceful", while the misty fog of sadness wafted through the furrows of my brain, like a morning haze in the mountains.

The answer to my pondering about the viability of these 9 Strategies, is a hearty and robust "yes". To borrow lamely from Rene Descartes, "I think, therefore I am" and to bring it relevance in the moment, I think better, therefore I am better.

I can't begin to imagine who I might have been had the experience of caregiving not shaped the last eight years of my life by these 9 Strategies. The simple act of noticing my life and applying ample amounts of awareness to it, has allowed creativity to take root, understanding to flourish, and contentment to grow. I always had an idea of who I was at my core, but was so distracted by the machinations of life that I never seemed to get around to sculpting the kind of life for myself that was reflective of that to the degree that it could be. But with my back pinned against the wall by the despair of this dreadful disease, I forged a plan to claw my way to mindfulness. We studied the methods that have worked for countless people over countless years and applied those methods to my circumstances. The simple acts of exploring solitude, contemplation, writing, reading, meditation, prayer, nourishment, exercise and passionate living, all became profound channels to put suffering in a broader context.

When you can see something for what it is, it can fuel the flames of growth and healing. It becomes something you can bring to the front and center of your awareness and create something extraordinary out of. Caregiving is exactly that. An opportunity where there once was a crushing weight. There is difference between being sad and having sadness. Having sadness is an appropriate and healthy emotion for the loss of a Loved One, where being sad can become a crushing ball and chain around your ankles preventing you from moving forward into a healthy and productive life.

Choose to be mindful, diligent and willing and you will prevail as a compassionate and healthy caregiver. We will emerge from this experience with stories to tell and more importantly, we will inform and inspire others who are lost in the quagmire of being a caregiver.

Take a walk today, or look expectantly into the faces of those around you, or just sit still on your bed upon waking…but feel deeply the open space of possibility as it has taken root inside of you. Become humble and obedient to the will of your divine nature as it speaks to you from within.

Move forward, seek peace and contentment within your heart, with a resolve for a profound and joyful experience of life. Do this for yourself and your Loved One.

Epilogue

Linda passed away on February 18th, 2017. She struggled until the end, her hold on life was so strong. The morning after she died, I stood over the vacant shell of her body and I wept deeply. I promised her I would do my best to live a good life and I asked her to keep an eye on me, and perhaps help me find my way if I wander off the trail.

We had a beautiful memorial service for her which opened with our dear friend Erica playing "Here, There and Everywhere" by the Beatles, the very same song she played at our wedding, bringing us full circle.

When it was my time to speak at the service, I made it clear that I wanted this day to be symbolic of turning the page on this last chapter of Linda's life. We no longer wanted to define her by this dreadful illness, but rather, move forward into the freedom of keeping her in our hearts in the free and unfettered way in which she lived her life. She was, after all, free and unburdened and I asked of myself and those in attendance to feel the freedom of this lifted burden as well.

That evening, I fell asleep in seconds, emotionally spent. When I awoke the next day, I felt a peace that I had not felt in years, and I continue to experience it.

I am ready for whatever comes next, and while I savor this moment, I will create a future for myself that will be a testament and a legacy to a great woman and the love we shared as well as a way to honor the gift of life that I was given.

It is to my sweet Linda, that this book is dedicated.

About the Authors

Dr. David Davis has been a chiropractor since 1982. His practice has been dedicated to serving the health care needs of his patients in Ridgefield, Connecticut. In addition, he has a profound love for educating people on the transformative principles of health and wellness, whether it is one on one, speaking to large groups, or in his writing. He also loves spending time in nature and traveling to the lesser visited places on the map.

As co-founder of Support the Caregiver, he continues to write and blog on Caregiving as a Possibility for Growth and Healing. He conducts seminars on the 9 Strategies for caregivers and health professionals. His writing has appeared in *Chicken Soup for the Soul, Living with Alzheimer's and other Dementias*. He has also spoken on behalf of the Alzheimer's Association,

He is currently traveling around the country with his dog Wally.

While Wally did not contribute to this book, it should be noted that he is a very good dog!

Joko Gilbert became involved in caregiving as a very close friend of Linda's. She saw the responsibilities and burdens involved and felt a strong calling to participate in a deeply committed way. Joko has spent much of her life in the study and practice of the healing art Reiki and nutrition and successfully completed the Alzheimer's Association's Dementia Care Training. For the past eight years, she has immersed herself in caring for Linda and David and continues to dedicate her work to Caregiver's and their Loved ones with Alzheimer's disease and took her involvement to the level of making it her life's work. As the founding partner of Support the Caregiver, she has developed a service dedicated to consulting caregivers and their families and friends, in how to successfully apply the 9 Strategies. She also offers a comprehensive online store, bringing the most impactful products to the people whose lives have been affected by this illness. One of her primary goals is to bring the Support the Caregiver seminars to as many caregivers as possible.

Joko resides in New York City with her two sons and husband.

A Note About <u>**Support the Caregiver**</u>
from Joko

David and I created the 9 Strategies of Support the Caregiver because my dear friend Linda was diagnosed with Early Onset Alzheimer's at the sweet age of 50. We needed a plan, we needed something to hold on to, something that elevated the challenge, the experience of being a caregiver, to something greater than just getting through it.

Observing Linda's husband David, I realized just how much support is necessary to deal with the at times overwhelming daily challenges of being the primary caregiver. David and Linda are my close friends, they are family. After Linda's diagnoses and after my initial shock eased a bit, I realized I had a choice to make. I could go on with life as I knew it. I could wait and see how the illness progressed and somehow down the road figure out how to support my friends when things got really tough. In my research I learned that David and Lin were going to need all the help they could get and that's when I made a promise to myself that I would be there for them 100 % and support them as best I could.

It was not easy! We struggled, a lot! We learned, we cried and thank goodness we remembered how to laugh! After 8 years of lovingly caring for Linda she passed on February 8th 2017.

My role during during the 8 years of caring for Linda evolved, sometimes daily. At first it was just about letting them know that I am there, any time of the day. It was about spending time together, cooking dinners, going for walks. It was my way of showing David and Linda that they were not alone. Then it became about sharing how to care for a women when she is no longer able to do so herself. As Linda's illness progressed I began to focus more and more on David. It was he, it seemed to me, that was suffering the most. Linda was happy, she was so well taken care of and quite unaware of all the worrying we did about her. David on the other hand showed serious signs of way too much stress. His heart was acting up, he became withdrawn and some days struggled with depression. He tried to comfort himself with foods that aggravated his heart and increased his girth. He stopped exercising. He didn't sleep. He felt trapped. He was grumpy. Sound familiar? I missed the David that could always make me laugh! And to make matters even worse, Linda wasn't happy when David wasn't happy.

Losing Linda to Alzheimer's disease was inevitable , and there was nothing I could do about it. I was not going to lose David too! *That* I could do something about! I became his caregiver, checking in with him numerous times daily on the phone or FaceTime. I became his sounding board, we figured out what works and what doesn't work caring for Linda and putting some focus back on his mental, physical and spiritual health. Gently and often I would encourage him to take care of his health, spruce up his eating habits, teach him how to cook healthier, spend time with him and Linda on FaceTime and in person during the most difficult times of the day. The difficulties did not always arise because of Linda, often it was David's lack of sleep, lack of alone time and deep sorrow that was the culprit for difficult times. The bottom line is, every primary caregiver, EVERY primary caregiver, needs a support system. It takes friends, family, neighbors, clergy, strangers! For the primary caregiver to go through this tremendously difficult time with their Loved One *and* remain healthy, physically, emotionally and spiritually, he (or she) must have support! My mission is to help create that support system for every primary caregiver caring for their Loved One afflicted with Alzheimer's disease. I can honestly say that these past 8 years have been the most heart wrenching of my life and I can also honestly say, with a heart filled with love and gratitude, that I am honored that David and Linda allowed me into their lives and hearts during this time with such openness and trust.

Support the Caregiver was created as a means to recognize the possibilities that come from adversity, and even discover how we can navigate through this challenging time and turn it into a growth experience. Support the Caregiver was created for you, the caregiver, that each and every morning gets up and cares for their Loved One, come what may. We know how hard it is at times and we want you to know that you are not alone and that you can emerge whole, healthy and with a peaceful mind. For us, this is about nothing less.

Please visit us and become part of the Support the Caregiver community at:

SupporttheCaregiver.com

Feel free to email us with any questions you might have at Joko@SupporttheCaregiver.com

"Life can only be understood backwards, but it must be lived forwards" - Søren Kierkergaard

What if?

Made in the USA
Middletown, DE
07 May 2017